This Storybook Bible
Belongs to:

_____

In the
Beginning

My Storybook Bible

Written by
Jonathan Shmidt Chapman

Illustrated by
César Garcés

For Amitai — I hope these tales will ignite your imagination and help
you see yourself in the ancient stories of our people.

In loving memory of Adam Shmidt z"l — who climbed to the tops of
mountains to catch a glimpse of the infinite.
— JSC

Apples & Honey Press
An Imprint of Behrman House Publishers
Millburn, New Jersey 07041
www.applesandhoneypress.com

ISBN 978-1-68115-689-7

Library of Congress Cataloging-in-Publication Data
Names: Chapman, Jonathan Shmidt, author. | Garcés, César, illustrator.
Title: In the beginning : my storybook Bible / by Jonathan Shmidt Chapman ;
illustrated by Cesar Garces.
Description: Millburn, New Jersey : Apples & Honey Press, 2024. | Audience:
Ages 4-7 | Audience: Grades K-1 | Summary: "Thirty stories from the Old
Testament retold to emphasize age-appropriate values, inclusivity, and a
progressive approach to religion"-- Provided by publisher.
Identifiers: LCCN 2023057898 | ISBN 9781681156897 (hardcover)
Subjects: LCSH: Bible stories, English--Old Testament--Juvenile literature.
Classification: LCC BS551.3 .C44 2024 | DDC 220.95/05--dc23/eng/20240202
LC record available at https://lccn.loc.gov/2023057898

Background images courtesy of Shutterstock: Jannarong: Pages 6; Gabriyel Onat: 48-49; Buzina
Svitlana: 50-51, 96-97, 104-105, 124-139, 142-145, 148-149, 158-159; Hanna0402: 64-67, 102-103,
114-115; A-Star: 76-77, 98-99; William Potter: 81-82; Colorful Freedom: 90-91, Flas 100: 100-101,
106-107, 122-123, endpapers; Myroshnichenko Violetta: 150-155.

Design by Book Buddy Media
Edited by Deborah Bodin Cohen
Printed in China

1 3 5 7 9 8 6 4 2

Jump right in!

This book is your very own storybook Bible.

It is filled with stories from a long, long, long time ago. They have been passed down from grown-ups to children for thousands of years.

And now it's your turn.

Listen closely. Do you hear them? The characters are jumping off the page. The stories are eagerly waiting to be told. They want to meet you.

Are you ready? Turn on your imagination, and jump inside of the Bible.

It's time. Here we go!

Table of Contents

Introduction

In the beginning . . . there were stories. The tales told in this book are thousands of years old and provide the foundation for three of the world's major religions. They have captivated storytellers and listeners around campfires, in places of worship, across dinner tables, and under covers at bedtime for generations. They are filled with epic journeys, family dramas, and awe-inspiring wonders. These stories are larger than life. And yet, even the youngest child can see themselves represented in the lessons that unfold through these narratives—learning to share, navigating big feelings like jealousy, taking care of the people you love, and recognizing the importance of home.

In the Beginning provides an introduction to the stories of the Bible—from the spark of Creation in Genesis to the Israelites preparing for the Promised Land in Deuteronomy—designed especially for young children and their families. While the tellings remain true to the source text, the adaptations focus on the characters and values that are most relevant and accessible to young readers.

Let There Be Everything

Before everything was created, there was . . . nothing. It was very quiet and still.

At the very beginning, God created light. A radiant spark shone through the darkness. It lit up the nothing with bright rays glowing everywhere.

The next day, God sculpted the sky and filled it with soft clouds. They floated gently and gleamed in the light.

Soon, the Earth was formed. Green plants sprouted from the ground, and trees stretched up out of the dirt.

Then, God hung the sun and the moon in the sky, and stars blinked throughout the galaxy.

God saw that it was good . . . but something was still missing. There were no creatures to fill the seas, or stretch across the sky, or crawl upon the Earth.

God made fish to swim in the seas, whales to glide across the oceans, and dolphins to splash through the waves.

Birds flew through the air, spreading their feathered wings and soaring overhead.

God created every kind of animal to roam the Earth. They had tails, and wings, and claws, and scales. Some liked the heat, and some liked the cold. Some burrowed deep underground and some built homes high up in the trees.

Finally on the sixth day, humans like you were made.

Now, God saw that it was very good. After all of that creating, God decided to take a day to rest. All of God's creations, no matter how big or small, closed their eyes and rested too. The busy Earth was quiet, peaceful, and still.

Adam and Eve Take A Bite

Adam and Eve lived in a beautiful place called the Garden of Eden. The sun shone brightly above them, and colorful wildflowers covered the ground. Wild animals ran through the fields. Birds soared through the sky and sang sweet songs in the trees.

As Adam and Eve saw each animal for the first time, they gave it a name. Adam looked up at a

large gray creature with floppy ears and a long trunk. "I will call you . . . elephant!" he said.

An animal with four legs galloped by, covered in black and white stripes. "Hmm . . . I think we'll name you . . . zebra!" Eve called out.

She looked down at a long creature slithering at her feet. "And you will be known as . . . snake," she said.

God told Adam and Eve that they could eat
fruit from any tree except for one—the Tree of
Knowledge. It stood tall in the middle of the
garden. Bright red fruit hung from its branches.

"Hiss, hiss . . . doesn't that apple look delicious?"
the snake whispered to Eve.

The fruit did look juicy and sweet, but God told her not to eat it. She repeated the snake's word, "delicious." She took a bite. It was the sweetest fruit she had ever tasted. She gave the apple to Adam and he took a bite too. Before they could take a second bite, everything changed.

In an instant, Eve and Adam grew up. They knew that the world had both good and bad things, right and wrong. God said, "You didn't listen to me. Now that you know more, you can't go back to before. You'll need to work like grownups, and you won't be able to stay and play in the garden all day."

Adam and Eve walked out of the garden, their eyes open to the vast and mysterious world around them.

Noah and the Fierce Flood

One day, a farmer named Noah was feeding his animals when he heard the voice of God: "Noah, are you listening? A big flood is coming! Water will soon cover the whole Earth. Get ready now!"

Noah quickly ran home to tell his wife Naamah. "We've got to do something before the flood comes," Noah said.

He and Naamah built a gigantic boat called an ark to protect their family from the storm. They invited two of every animal to board the ark with them. A pair of giraffes strolled gracefully up the ramp. Two excited bunnies quickly hopped past

them, while a duo of turtles slowly crawled
behind. Hundreds of animals paraded on
to the ark, eager to find a
spot before the flood
waters came.

As Noah was closing the ark's door, Naamah felt something wet fall onto her head.

"Did you feel that?" she asked.

The drop became a drizzle, and the drizzle became a downpour. As the flood waters covered everything in sight, Noah, Naamah, their family, and the animals were safe inside the ark. They floated on the water for forty days and forty nights.

When the rain finally stopped, Noah looked out of the windows of the ark and saw water in all directions. He sent a dove to see if any of the land was dry. The dove returned with an olive branch.

"The day we've been waiting for has finally arrived," Noah shouted joyfully as he showed the branch of fresh green leaves to the animals. "Plants are growing again. It's time to open the door!"

As Noah and his family walked out of the ark onto dry land, they squinted into the bright sunny sky and noticed something remarkable.

The world's first rainbow stretched out above them—a promise that after every storm comes peaceful beautiful light.

The Tower of Babel

After the flood, all of the people on Earth lived close together in one very crowded city. They spoke the same language, celebrated the same holidays, ate the same foods, and even listened to the same music.

As the city grew, it became more and more cramped. One day, someone had an idea.

"Why don't we build up? Then we can have more space."

"We can extend our city into the sky!" another agreed.

The people started to build. They built a tower that grew

taller,

and

taller,

and

taller.

"Maybe we can build our tower so high that it will reach all the way up to God!" someone said. All the people cheered.

God saw the people building and heard their plans. "The people are trying to reach the heavens and me," said God with concern. "The people should spread out across the beautiful Earth and make it their home. I need to do something."

And so God did. Suddenly the people spoke many different languages. They couldn't understand each other. They wanted to learn new things and live in different places.

"I want to live by the ocean," said one person.

"I want to live by the mountains!" said his friend in a different language.

Unable to understand each other, the two friends ran in different directions.

The people stopped building their tower. Instead, they spread out, starting new towns and cities. People in each place celebrated their own holidays, invented new recipes, and composed new music.

The people realized that the world was a much more interesting place this way. And God did too.

5

Abraham and Sarah's Big Adventure

One night, a shepherd named Abraham looked at the sun setting behind the mountains in the distance. He was just about to say goodnight to all his sheep, when he heard the voice of God say: "Go forth!"

"Go . . . where?" Abraham wondered.

"It's time for you to travel far away to a new land. It's time to start a new adventure," said God.

This could have been a scary command, but Abraham trusted God. "Go forth . . . okay!" he thought as he ran back to his tent.

Abraham found his wife Sarah and told her about
hearing God. He asked, "What do you think?
Our family is here, this is our home."

"Don't worry," Sarah said calmly. "It won't be easy to leave this place but no matter where we go, as long as we're together, it will feel like home."

God promised Abraham and Sarah that their family would grow and grow and grow, filling the world with love, stories, and tradition. Abraham and Sarah agreed that God's plan sounded like a wonderful adventure. Early the next morning, they packed up the tent, told the sheep it was time to go, and set off into the unknown.

They hiked across hot sand, waded through a rushing river, and climbed steep hills.

"We're almost there, I can see it up ahead," Sarah said.

Finally, they reached the land of Canaan. "This is it," said Abraham.

"We're home," said Sarah, smiling.

6

Hagar and the Wonderful Wish

Sarah and Abraham loved their new home in Canaan. Just one thing was missing. They dreamed of having a child. They wished and hoped, but no baby arrived.

One morning, Sarah felt especially sad. "What is bothering you?" said Hagar, a kind-hearted woman who worked for her.

Sarah explained her troubles to Hagar. She said, "I think we need some help."

"I'll have a baby for you, and we'll build a family together," Hagar said.

Not too long afterward, Hagar came running over to Sarah and said, "Our dreams are coming true. I'm going to have a baby!"

Sarah wanted to be happy, but she only felt jealous. "Why is Hagar the one having the baby instead of me?" Sarah thought to herself.

Sarah spoke harshly to Hagar and gave her twice as much work as before.

"I can't take this anymore," thought Hagar. "I need to run away." She walked and walked in the hot sun, finally stopping to take a drink of water.

An angel found Hagar by a spring of water. "Where are you going?" asked the angel.

"I just had to leave. Sarah was treating me unkindly."

"Go back home to the camp," the angel said. "You will soon have a baby boy. Name him Ishmael, which means God heard you. Your son will become a leader, and your family will grow and grow."

Hagar smiled, imagining all of the ways her baby would make a difference in the world. She got up and walked home.

Soon, the tent was filled with the sound that Hagar, Abraham, and Sarah had dreamed of hearing: a baby cooing with joy.

7

Sarah and the Welcoming Tent

At the end of a very hot day, Sarah rested inside the family tent, trying to escape from the sweltering sun. As she prepared to take a nap, she heard the tired footsteps of travelers walking by.

"Excuse me, my friends . . . do you need a place to rest?" she heard Abraham call out to them.

Although she was exhausted from the day's heat, Sarah didn't want to pass up the chance to be welcoming to fellow travelers.

"Come in! Our tent is open on all sides. We'll take care of you," Sarah called out.

She poured cups of fresh water for the three guests, while Abraham bathed their feet. Then, Sarah baked fresh bread and Abraham prepared the meat.

Their bellies full, the guests prepared to leave. "We can't thank you enough!" said one guest. "You will be blessed for being so generous. You will soon become parents and welcome a child into the world."

Sarah laughed out loud. "What?! That's not possible. Abraham and I are much too old to have a baby now."

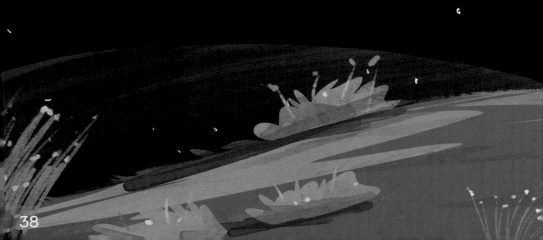

But the mysterious guests were right,
and Abraham welcomed a son into th
They named him Isaac, which means
and their tent grew bigger. As she hel
underneath the twinkling stars, Sarah
the three guests and filled the quiet n
joyful laughter.

8

Rebecca and the Thirsty Camels

Rebecca grew up in the quiet town of Haran. Every morning, she drew water from the well. "One day, I'll leave this place and see more of the world!" she promised herself.

Meanwhile, across the desert, Isaac dreamed of finding a partner to explore the world with him. "It's lonely here in my tent," Isaac thought.

Abraham knew his son was lonely and asked his assistant Eliezer for help. "Can you go out and look for a good partner for Isaac?" asked Abraham.

As the sun rose, Eliezer left on his journey, taking ten camels with him. He traveled for many days across the desert.

Many mornings later, Rebecca saw Eliezer and ten very tired camels laying out in the hot sun. "Do you need help?" she called.

"Water . . . please . . . " Eliezer whispered.

Rebecca worked quickly. She first brought a jug of water for Eliezer to drink. Then, she drew jug after jug of water for his camels.

Rebecca invited Eliezer back to her family's house and made fresh pita and salad for him. As they ate, Rebecca listened to Eliezer tell stories about life in Haran. Her eyes lit up with wonder.

Eliezer had an idea. "Rebecca, you have shown so much kindness, giving me food and a place to rest," Eliezer said. "Would you like to travel with me to meet my friend Isaac? I think you and he would really get along."

Rebecca felt a rush of excitement. She could leave Haran, meet Isaac, and explore the world. Her life could be more than drawing water from a well and tending to sheep. "Yes, I'll go," she said.

Her family didn't want her to leave but, when they saw she was eager for the adventure, they gave their blessing and helped her pack for the trip. She kissed them all goodbye, climbed onto a camel, and left to find adventure beyond her watering well.

9

Brothers and
the Birthright

Isaac and Rebecca loved each other from the moment they saw each other. They went on many adventures together, riding their camels and exploring the wilderness beyond their tent. In time, they became parents to twin sons.

The two boys couldn't have been more different. Jacob was quiet, organized, and liked to stay home. Esau never planned anything; he was wild, messy, and liked the wilderness. Esau was born just a few moments before Jacob, so he got special privileges for being the first born, called a birthright. When the family traveled, Esau got to ride the first camel in the caravan. When guests visited, Isaac always introduced Esau first. This made Jacob jealous.

One day, Esau was tired and hungry after playing outside. He smelled something delicious. "What are you cooking?" he asked, watching as Jacob stirred a big bowl of stew.

"Red lentil stew. It's almost ready," Jacob said.

"Give me a bowl. I am starving!" Esau said.

Jacob considered Esau's request. "You can have my stew . . . but I want your birthright in return."

Esau's stomach was growling. What good was his birthright when he was so hungry? "You can take my birthright, just give me something to eat," said Esau.

Esau gobbled up the stew but, once his belly was full, he realized what he had done.

"Jacob! You tricked me! I want my birthright back!"

But it was too late. "You knew what you were doing," said Jacob with a smirk. "A deal is a deal."

10

Jacob Takes the Blessing

When Isaac grew old and he could barely see anymore, he called his older son Esau to his tent.

"I'm getting older, and it is time for us to plan for the future," Isaac told him. "Cook me my favorite meal and I'll give you a blessing to be the next leader of our family. As the eldest, you will take my place."

Rebecca overheard them talking. Although she loved both her sons, she thought Jacob would make a better family leader.

"Your dad is about make Esau the new leader for our family," Rebecca whispered to Jacob. "You would make a much better leader. The role of family leader should be yours. I'll help you get it."

Rebecca cooked Isaac's favorite meal, then helped Jacob dress like Esau. "Come here, put this on," she said to Jacob, handing him a fuzzy sweater that belonged to Esau. "It will feel like Esau's hairy arms."

Dressed like his brother, Jacob carried the steaming meal to Isaac's tent.

"Who is at the door with my favorite food?" Isaac asked.

"It is your son, Esau," Jacob pretended. He put out his arm for Isaac to feel, tricking his dad into thinking he was his brother.

Issac ate the meal and gave Jacob his blessing to lead the family.

When Esau returned to camp, he realized what his brother had done. "Jacob!? I can't believe you tricked me again!"

Afraid of what Esau might do to him, Jacob ran far away into the wilderness. He set off in the direction of Haran, his mother's childhood home, hoping to find a welcoming place to rest.

11

Jacob and the Ladder to the Sky

"Just keep running," Jacob said to himself, out of breath as he sped across the desert. He ran far away from home, afraid of what his brother Esau might do to him for taking both his birthright and blessing.

After traveling as far as his feet could take him, Jacob stopped in the wilderness to rest for the night. He found a quiet

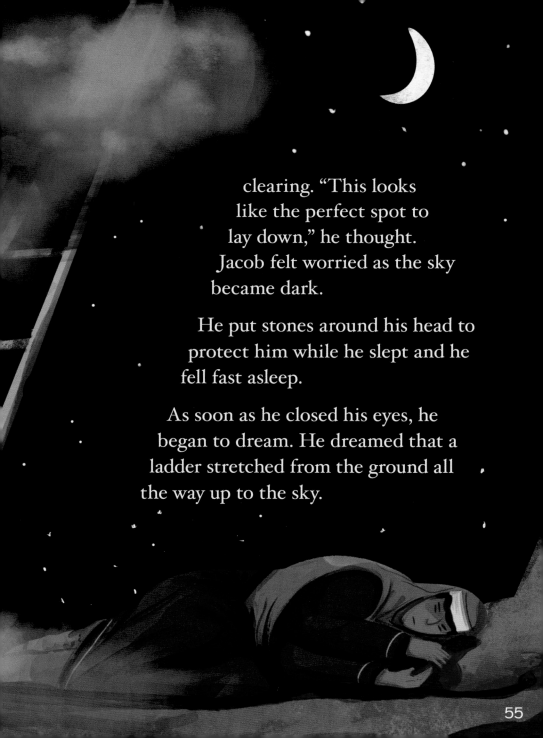

clearing. "This looks
like the perfect spot to
lay down," he thought.
Jacob felt worried as the sky
became dark.

He put stones around his head to
protect him while he slept and he
fell fast asleep.

As soon as he closed his eyes, he
began to dream. He dreamed that a
ladder stretched from the ground all
the way up to the sky.

As Jacob looked up, he saw angels traveling up and down the ladder. He heard God's voice saying, "I will be with you, and I will protect you wherever you go. You will not be alone, and your family will grow and grow to spread across the world."

When Jacob woke up, he didn't feel afraid anymore. "It's time for me to stop running and make a new home," he thought.

He continued on his journey, and finally arrived in Haran—the same city where his mother Rebecca grew up and where his grandparents Sarah and Abraham had lived.

He noticed the well at the center of town and remembered the stories that Rebecca used to tell him as a child.

"This is the place where my mother showed kindness and helped others get water," Jacob said as he sat at the well and took a drink. "Maybe I will find a kind and loving home here too."

12

Rachel and Leah Work Together

Rachel and her older sister Leah lived on a hill in Haran with their father Laban. Every day, they took care of the family's flock. One afternoon, Rachel was tending the sheep when she saw a man approaching. "Leah, who is that man coming down the path?" asked Rachel.

"I've not seen him before," answered Leah.

When Jacob got close, he saw Rachel and Leah needed help giving water to the sheep.

"I can help you!" Jacob said. He looked at Rachel and knew right away that he wanted to get to know her better.

Their father Laban came out of his tent to see what all the fuss was about.

"You are my sister Rebecca's son. Welcome to my home!" said Laban. He offered Jacob a job and a place to stay. Jacob agreed to work for Laban and tend to his flocks.

Jacob spent all his free time with Rachel. They hiked, played board games, and talked about the future. Soon, Jacob and Rachel fell in love. Laban agreed they could marry once Jacob worked for seven years.

At the end of the seventh year, Jacob said to Laban, "It is time for your daughter and me to finally get married. We want to start a family."

"Of course!" Laban said.

The day of the wedding arrived. Jacob walked
under the wedding canopy and saw the bride
standing in front of him, her face covered with a
veil. He smiled. After the wedding, Jacob lifted his
bride's veil . . . and it was Leah!

"You tricked me, Laban!" Jacob said.

"The older sister must marry first," Laban declared. "But you can marry Rachel too, if you promise to work for me for another seven years."

After Jacob married Rachel, Leah felt jealous. But as time passed, Leah and Rachel grew close once again.

Many years later, Rachel and Leah watched their twelve children running around in the starlit night. They remembered Jacob telling them of God's promise of a large family. "It came true!" they said with smiles.

63

13

The Reunion of the Brothers

Jacob couldn't sleep. His son Levi was snoring, his son Ruben kept sneezing, and his sons Dan and Judah could not stop giggling. His family needed a bigger tent. "It's time for us to move," Jacob said to Leah and Rachel. "Let's pack up and bring the family to Canaan, where I grew up. We can spread out there."

Jacob wanted to see his childhood home after all these years, but he felt nervous about seeing his brother Esau again. "Will he still be mad at me for taking his birthright and blessing when we were younger?" Jacob wondered. "I need to make things right."

He sent a messenger to Esau, and he waited and waited. Would Esau agree to see him again?

Finally, Esau sent a message: "Let's meet, brother."

"What if he won't forgive me?" Jacob asked Rachel and Leah.

"Leah and I sometimes fight, but we always make up in the end," said Rachel.

"It is never too late to apologize," Leah added.

During the days leading up to their reunion, Jacob prepared a gift for his brother, hoping to show Esau he was sorry for everything.

The morning of the reunion had finally arrived. As the sun came up, Jacob saw Esau walking toward him, his family at his side. Jacob slowly and carefully took a step forward. Then Esau took a step forward. They stopped and held their breath, waiting to see what the other would do. To Jacob's surprise, Esau ran to greet him. Esau threw his arms around Jacob and hugged him. The brothers were finally reunited.

14

Joseph and His Wild Dreams

Jacob loved all of his thirteen children, but Joseph was his favorite. Jacob gave Joseph a unique and eye-catching gift. "Joseph, try on this beautiful coat decorated with many colors. It's one of a kind, just like you," Jacob said.

All of Joseph's brothers were very jealous. "Why does he get a fancy coat? What's so special about him anyway?" they grumbled.

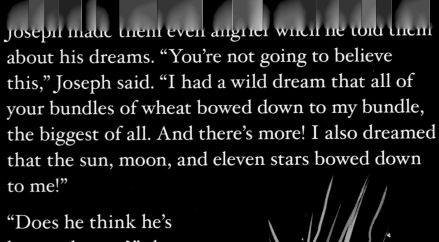

Joseph made them even angrier when he told them about his dreams. "You're not going to believe this," Joseph said. "I had a wild dream that all of your bundles of wheat bowed down to my bundle, the biggest of all. And there's more! I also dreamed that the sun, moon, and eleven stars bowed down to me!"

"Does he think he's better than us?" the brothers grumbled, getting more jealous with each day.

One day, as the brothers worked in the fields, they decided to get rid of Joseph once and for all. "What are you all doing?" Joseph said when he noticed his brothers all whispering to each other. Before he knew what was happening, they tore off his beautiful coat.

"Quick! Throw him in that pit!" one of the brothers shouted. They pushed Joseph into a deep hole in the ground. Just then, a caravan of traders rode by.

"Let's sell him to those traders, and send him far away," suggested another brother.

They sold Joseph as a slave for twenty pieces of silver. The brothers watched as the traders loaded Joseph into their wagon and left, traveling in the direction of Egypt.

When the brothers returned home, Jacob looked around and saw that Joseph was missing. "Where is Joseph?" he asked his children.

"He's gone for good, lost in the wilderness!" they cried.

Jacob was heartbroken.

Meanwhile, Joseph arrived in the land of Egypt,
far away from home and unsure if he would ever
see his family again.

15

Joseph Has A Plan

Pharaoh, the king of Egypt, had a mysterious dream one night. "I dreamed that seven skinny cows ate seven fat cows. What could it mean?" he cried out. "Find someone who can figure this out!"

Pharaoh's advisors heard about a man who could explain the meaning of dreams. They found the man and brought him into the throne room. "What is your name, young man?" said Pharaoh, staring down at him.

"My name is Joseph, your majesty," he said nervously.

Pharaoh recounted his dream, then said impatiently, "Well . . . what are you waiting for? Tell me what my dream means!"

"Pharaoh, Egypt will have seven years filled with crops growing across the land, followed by seven years when nothing will grow," said Joseph. "That's what the seven fat cows and seven skinny cows mean."

Pharaoh heard Joseph's warning and shook with fear. "What am I going to do to save my people? Joseph, I need your help. Join my royal team of advisors, and make a plan to save us!" Pharaoh demanded.

During the seven years of plentiful crops, Joseph helped store lots of food, so that Egypt had enough when food became hard to find. During the seven years of famine, the Egyptians had enough to eat, thanks to Joseph. But, outside Egypt, people were not as lucky.

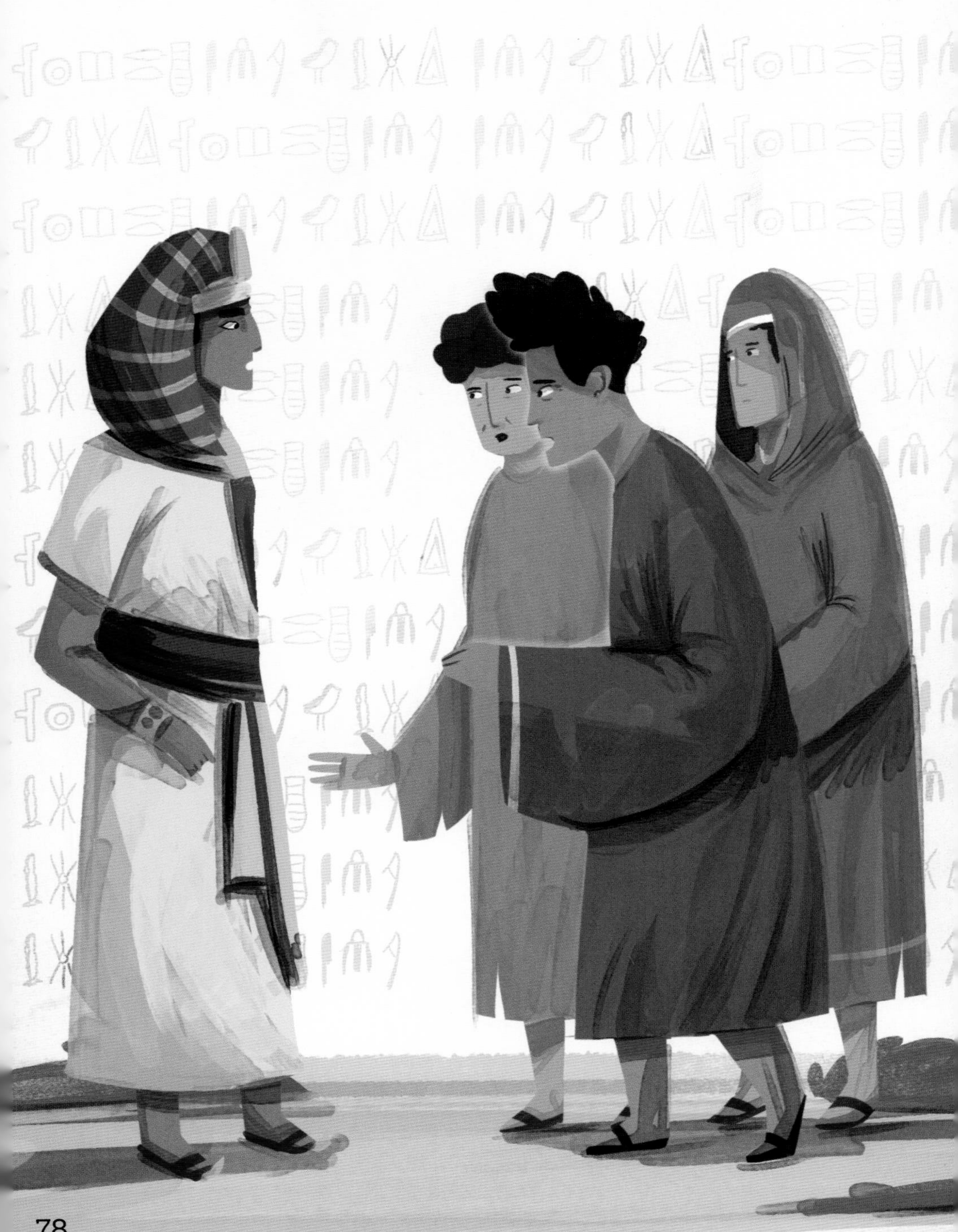

In Canaan, Joseph's family struggled to eat when the food ran out. "What are we going to do? We're so hungry!" Joseph's brothers groaned.

"I hear that there's still food in Egypt," Jacob told them. "Go there and find us something to eat."

When the brothers arrived in Egypt, Joseph recognized them right away. But Joseph's brothers didn't recognize him. They thought that he was an Egyptian prince. Joseph decided to test his brothers to see if they had changed. "You'll be my guests for dinner!" Joseph announced.

Joseph had a plan. He would hide a beautiful cup in his youngest brother Benjamin's bag. When the cup was found there, Joseph would tell his guards to take Benjamin away to jail. Would the brothers let him go, or would they speak up to protect him?

16

The Case of the Stolen Cup

Judah sat at a long table with his ten brothers and their host—the Egyptian prince. "Why did this prince invite his family to dine with him?" Judah wondered as he enjoyed a plate piled high with olives, pita, fresh fish, and cucumber salad. Back home, there was nothing to eat, and his family was hungry all the time.

After filling their bellies, the brothers were getting ready to leave when they heard a booming voice. The Egyptian prince called out, "Wait! My special cup is missing! Guards, check their bags!"

The guards rummaged through their bags. Judah and his brothers stood frozen, then gasped when the guards found the cup in their youngest brother Benjamin's bag.

What would happen to Benjamin? Judah knew he could not leave Benjamin behind. Judah hadn't stood up for Joseph all those years ago, but he could still help Benjamin. He bravely stepped forward. "Don't take Benjamin. Take me instead."

The Egyptian prince started to cry. "Brothers, don't you see? It's me, Joseph!"

Judah was in shock. His long-lost brother was standing right in front of him. Judah felt ashamed for what he and his brothers had done to Joseph. "I see you've changed since you tricked me," Joseph said.

Joseph hugged his brothers. "Go tell father that I'm here," Joseph said. "Bring him to Egypt."

The brothers returned home to share the news. Judah said, "Father, we found Joseph! He helped Pharaoh save everyone."

Jacob couldn't believe it. "I have to see him, right

away!" Judah helped Jacob pack up all his things, and the family moved to Egypt.

"Joseph . . . is that really you?" Jacob said with tears in his eyes. Jacob held Joseph in a hug for a long time, then shouted for everyone to hear, "My children are all together again."

17

Shifra and Puah Save the Day

Many, many good years passed in Egypt. Jacob's children had many children. The family grew into twelve tribes called the Israelites.

A new Pharaoh came to power in Egypt. This Pharaoh didn't know about Joseph. "The Israelites must work for me," he declared. "They are my slaves now, and they will build my cities, brick by brick."

The Israelites worked in the hot sun for Pharaoh, building all day without any breaks. Even though life was hard in Egypt, the Israelites kept having more and more babies.

Two Israelite midwives, Shifra and Puah, went from tent to tent, helping Israelite women when their babies were ready to be born. "Let's go, we need to help another family bring their baby into the world. We're going to be late!" Shifra said to Puah.

Shifra and Puah loved taking care of the babies, but their job was sad too. "I wish you didn't have to grow up here in Egypt as a slave," Puah said looking down at a wide-eyed baby in her arms.

One day, Pharaoh demanded Shifra and Puah come to the palace.

"There are too many Israelites. Someday they might try to go free. Starting today, there can be no more new Israelite baby boys in Egypt," he told Shifra and Puah. "I command: When a baby boy is born, get rid of him!"

But Shifra and Puah were brave. "We must help the children," said Puah.

"We'll hide the baby boys and take care of them without the Pharaoh finding out," said Shifra.

Every time they helped deliver a baby boy, Shifra and Puah hid him from the palace guards.

"There's hope, little one. Pharaoh's cruel ways will not last forever," said Puah to each baby. "One day, we will all be safe and free."

18

The Baby in the Basket

An Israelite woman named Yocheved rocked her son in her arms, trying to get him to fall asleep. She whispered softly, "Today is a big day, my love."

Most days, Yocheved worked for Pharaoh in the hot sun, making bricks out of mortar. But today was different. When Yocheved heard Pharaoh's decree to rid Egypt of Israelite baby boys, she knew she had to make a plan to keep her son safe.

"I will put you in a basket and send you down the Nile River," she whispered. "May you find a better place where you can be safe and free."

Yocheved told her daughter Miriam to
follow the basket and make sure the baby
had a safe journey. Miriam hid among the
tall reeds along the river.

The basket floated along the winding river
until it reached the center of the city. Pharaoh's
daughter Batya was taking a swim when she
noticed the basket. "There's a baby in
this basket!" she gasped. "Don't worry,
precious child, I will keep you safe.
I will name you Moses. It means
to 'take out of the water.'"

Miriam watched as Batya carried the baby into the palace. "Be brave, my brother," she whispered. "Have faith: One day we'll see each other again. And maybe, then, we'll both know what it means to be free."

19

The Burning Bush

Pharaoh's daughter raised Moses as an Egyptian prince. But deep in his heart, Moses felt like an Israelite. Living in Pharaoh's palace, Moses saw all the cruel things that Pharaoh did to the Israelites. He watched slaves lift heavy brick after heavy brick. They never took a break, even for a drink.

One afternoon, Moses saw an Egyptian taskmaster punish an Israelite slave for working too slowly. Moses had enough. "I can't live here while my people are slaves!"

Moses ran far away into the wilderness all the way to the land of Midian. The Midianite people treated each other kindly, like one loving family. "I could get used to life here," thought Moses.

He stayed and became a shepherd, caring for a
flock of sheep. In time, he married a shepherdess
named Zipporah and they had two sons.

One morning while Zipporah was cooking near their tent, she saw Moses running toward her. He was out of breath, and talking fast. "Slow down," she said. "What happened?"

"I saw something incredible: a bush was bright with fire, but the flame wasn't destroying the branches. Suddenly, I heard a voice from within the bush! I think it was the voice of God."

"What did God say?" Zipporah asked.

"God said to me: 'Moses—Return to Egypt, and tell Pharaoh to let my people go. I will be with you every step of the way.'"

"Leading others to freedom. This is your destiny, Moses," said Zipporah.

Moses was nervous, but he knew he had to help the Israelites. Zipporah helped him pack up his things and hugged him goodbye.

He began the long journey back to Egypt to free his people.

20

Let My People Go!

Moses walked across the desert toward Egypt. As Moses approached Egypt, God sent his brother Aaron to meet him. Aaron hugged his long-lost brother and said, "I knew you'd come back!"

Moses felt nervous. "I'm not good at giving speeches, I get tongue-tied. How will I confront Pharaoh?"

"Don't worry, I'll help you speak to Pharaoh," Aaron said. "Standing up to a bully is hard on your own. But we are stronger together. We're a team."

Together Moses and Aaron climbed the tall staircase to the palace. They walked straight into the throne room and up to Pharaoh. "Let my people go!" Moses said.

"They deserve to be free," added Aaron. "You can't force them to work for you anymore!"

"Absolutely not! The Israelites belong to me," Pharaoh said sternly.

Moses tried asking many times, but it was no use. Pharaoh just kept saying no. Moses started feeling discouraged.

"Remember what God told you from the burning bush," Aaron said.

"God said to me: 'I will be with you, helping you every step of the way,'" remembered Moses.

With some help from God, wild things started to happen in Egypt.

Moses put his staff in the waters of the Nile River, and it suddenly turned completely blood red.

More plagues followed. Millions of frogs appeared everywhere across the land, hopping on tables, in beds, and even in the palace!

Lice swarmed, wild animals roamed the streets, and hail fell from the sky.

Moses approached Pharaoh again and said, "God is telling you to let the Israelites go!"

But Pharaoh still refused.

21

Moses, Lead the Way!

"Pharaoh, let the Israelites go free!" Moses demanded again, hoping Pharaoh would change his mind. For too long, the Israelites had been slaves, working for Pharaoh without any choice.

Pharaoh crossed his arms, shook his head. "No, Moses. I will not let them go."

Moses sighed and said,
"Then God will make more
wild things happen to your people.
More plagues will come. You will see,
hear, and even taste God's power."

All of a sudden, swarms of locusts buzzed overhead.
It was so loud that the Egyptians couldn't hear each
other through the sounds of the flying insects.

Then, a total darkness covered the land of Egypt.
The Egyptians couldn't see their hands in front of
their faces, and they kept bumping into each other.
It was dark even at noon! All of Egypt shut down.

Pharaoh still refused to change his mind. So, even more terrible things happened. Finally, it was too much for Pharaoh. "Enough! Take your people and go!" roared Pharaoh.

This was it! The moment of freedom had arrived. The Israelites could hardly believe it. Were they really free to leave?

Moses told the Israelites to pack up very quickly and get ready to go. He saw some Israelites baking bread to take with them. "We must leave! There's no time to let the bread dough rise. Just bake the dough like it is."

The flat matzah bread tasted plain but so good. It was freedom bread. The Israelites packed it for the journey ahead. All together as one community, the Israelites followed Moses out of Egypt, finally on their way to freedom.

22

The Israelites and the Red Sea

"We're free!" Miriam said as the Israelites journeyed out of Egypt and into the wilderness. She smiled at her brother Moses as he led the way across the desert.

As the sun went down, Miriam and the rest of the Israelites froze in fear. They saw the waves of the Red Sea rising in front of them. Water stretched out as far as their eyes could see.

"How are we going to cross? What are we going to do now?!" Moses said to Miriam.

"Be brave and the people will be brave too," said Miriam.

Moses raised his staff over the water, and it suddenly parted into two walls, with a dry path in the middle for them to cross! As the Israelites walked down the path, they could see whales gliding, dolphins jumping, and jellyfish floating through the walls of the water.

"Brave Israelites: Grab your tambourines, and let's celebrate with a song!" Miriam said as they reached the other side. All the women danced and sang together.

The Israelites felt hungry after walking through the wilderness all day. They wondered what they would eat in the desert.

In the morning, Miriam peeked out of her tent and her eyes went wide. Covering the entire wilderness was a layer of food that had fallen from the sky. "What is this?" the people asked.

"This is a food called manna that God has given us to eat," Moses told them.

"It's okay to eat," reassured Miriam. The people bravely tried one bite of the new food and then another.

As Miriam enjoyed the delicious taste of the manna, she knew that the Israelites would be able to find their way through any problem big or small along the journey ahead. They were brave and strong. And free.

23

A Big Day at Sinai

After traveling the desert for seven weeks, the Israelites arrived at Mt. Sinai. "This is the spot," Moses told them. "Set up your tents and rest your feet, we'll be staying for a while. Here at Mount Sinai, we will get a gift: God's instructions for how we live together on our own as free people."

"Free people!" cheered the Israelites.

"I must leave you to climb the mountain. Keep your eyes and ears open," Moses said.

Suddenly, the sky filled with lighting, and fire and smoke appeared on top of the mountain.

A very loud blast was sounded, and the whole mountain shook and trembled. It was an incredible sight.

A cloud covered the mountain. "I am your God, who brought you out of Egypt," said God to Moses. Then, God announced the Ten Commandments, the most important rules and ideas the Israelites would need to follow.

1. I am your one and only God.

2. Don't create any sculptures or pictures to be your God.

3. Be careful with the words you use.

4. Make time to rest each week.

5. Respect your parents and caregivers.

6. Don't hurt other people.

7. Keep your promises to the people you love.

8. Don't take what isn't yours.

9. Don't tell lies.

10. Don't be jealous of other people.

The Israelites stood together, looking up at the mountain feeling wonder and thankfulness for all God had given them.

24

The Golden Calf

While Moses was inside of the cloud on top of Mount Sinai, the Israelites waited for him to return. And waited. And waited. They tried to be patient but began to worry. "What if Moses never comes back?"

As they got more and more nervous, they grew less and less patient. They decided they needed to build a new god. "Aaron, help us make a new god to lead us!" they pleaded.

Aaron wondered if the people were right. "Gather all of your gold and bring it to me!" Aaron declared.

The Israelites collected all their shiny gold, and
Aaron burned it down, sculpting it into a statue
of a golden calf. "This golden cow will be our new
god!" Aaron said.

The Israelites threw a wild party and danced around the statue all night. They were singing so loudly that they didn't notice Moses running down from the mountain.

"What do you think you are doing?! Why weren't you more patient?" Moses yelled down from the path, holding the two stone tablets with the Ten Commandments.

Moses was so angry that he threw the tablets to the ground, breaking them into pieces.

"Moses . . . we're so sorry. We don't know what we were thinking!" they cried.

"We were nervous that you still hadn't come back, and things just got out of hand," Aaron said, staring at their silly golden statue.

Moses went back up the mountain to get a new set of tablets. "Just be patient. I'll be back soon," Moses warned.

This time, the Israelites trusted that they just needed to wait and he would come back.

25

Bezalel Builds Something Beautiful

Moses stood at the base of the mountain, holding the new set of tablets with the Ten Commandments written on them. "Gather around everyone, it's time to build!" said Moses.

Bezalel loved to build things and ran over to listen.

"These tablets need a really safe place to hold them," said Moses. "We will build a temple that we can move with us through the desert. We'll call it the Tabernacle. It's going to take creativity, building skills and teamwork. Who can help?"

"This is my chance to make a difference!" thought Bezalel as he jumped in the air. He raised his hand and called out, "I can help!"

Bezalel became the chief builder of the Tabernacle. Using instructions from God, he planned out how to build the Tabernacle.

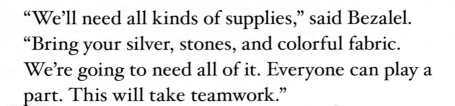

"We'll need all kinds of supplies," said Bezalel. "Bring your silver, stones, and colorful fabric. We're going to need all of it. Everyone can play a part. This will take teamwork."

All the Israelites wanted to help. They gathered all of the supplies for the project. Bezalel's team worked together day and night to create the Tabernacle, sharing ideas to make it a beautiful place.

"We can use these bright red, purple, and blue yarns to weave the curtains," shared a weaver.

"This beautiful wood can be used to create the poles for tent," said a carpenter.

They used the finest gold to build the Ark, a box where the Ten Commandments were kept safe.

"This is just right," Bezalel said as he hammered the final piece in place on the Ark. "I'm so lucky to have such a talented team. Great work, everyone!"

26

Adventures of the Scouts

After traveling through the wilderness for a long time, the Israelites set up a campsite on the opposite side of the Jordan River from the land of Canaan.

"We're getting close to Canaan," said Caleb.

"I think I can see it in the distance," replied Joshua as he squinted to see the land beyond the river. "Our new home."

"It's so close I can almost taste it!" said Caleb.

Moses sent twelve scouts, one person from each tribe, into the land to investigate and report back. Caleb and Joshua were chosen to be part of the mission. "I wonder what we'll find there," Joshua said to Caleb as they waved goodbye to the campsite.

After exploring Canaan, the scouts brought back giant grapes, pomegranates, and figs to show the people. The Israelites gathered around, eager to hear about their adventure and taste the fruit. "What did you find there?" asked one Israelite.

"Is it as wonderful as we imagine?" asked another.

"It is a beautiful land," reported Caleb.

"The land really does flow with milk and honey. It's amazing!" said Joshua.

But the rest of the scouts warned that giants lived in the land. "They were big and scary!" said one scout.

"They made us feel as tiny as grasshoppers!" said another.

Some Israelites shuddered. Some Israelites cried.

Caleb and Joshua tried to tell the Israelites that it would be okay, and that God would protect them when they went into Canaan. But the people were too scared to go.

Because they were so fearful, God decided the Israelites weren't ready to enter the land. "I can't believe it isn't time yet, we're so close to the land!" Joshua said to Caleb, disappointed that they couldn't settle down.

The Israelites would need to continue to travel through the desert for many more years until they were ready to build a home in Canaan.

27

Are We There Yet?

"Let's go, everyone! It's time to travel to the next campsite," Moses announced as the tired Israelites marched behind him.

As they walked and walked through the hot wilderness, the Israelites complained to Moses a lot about the journey. "Moses, we're so tired!" cried an Israelite.

"Moses, we're so thirsty!" whined another.

"Are we there yet?!" shouted a third.

Miriam had followed her brother through the wilderness for a long time, and even she was getting frustrated. "I'm so tired of not knowing where we're going or when we'll stop to rest!" Miriam thought, frowning at Moses.

As she listened to the complaints of the weary Israelites around her, Miriam felt angry that Moses got to make all of the decisions about their journey.

She grumbled angrily to Aaron, "Why does our brother think he always knows the right way to lead us? It isn't fair, there's nothing that special about him."

God heard Miriam and said, "It isn't nice to talk about your brother that way. You need to leave the camp and spend some time alone. Perhaps you'll understand why I chose Moses to lead."

Miriam moved her tent outside of the camp for seven days. She thought about what she said behind her brother's back, and she remembered all of the ways that her brother cared for the Israelites since they left Egypt. "No matter how tired or angry I get, I shouldn't speak out against my own brother. It must not be easy leading all of us through the wilderness," Miriam thought as she returned to camp.

Miriam saw how her brother kept calm
even as the people constantly complained.
She gave Moses a hug as the Israelites kept
moving toward the next campsite.

28

The Sisters Who Spoke Up

As they got closer to Canaan, all the Israelites talked excitedly about where they would live when they arrived. Moses had explained that each family would get a plot of land to call their own.

"Do you think we'll be able to live in a house soon, instead of this tent?" Hoglah asked her four sisters.

"I hope so," said her sister Noa. "I can't wait to build our beautiful house."

Even though their father Zelophehad was no longer living, Hoglah, Noa, and their three other sisters—Milcah, Mahlah, and Tirzah—planned to build a family home together. Noa said, "We'll remember our father every day when we build a house on the land that would have been his."

Their neighbor overheard the sisters talking. "Don't you know, your father's land can only be passed down to a son?" said the neighbor. "That's the rule. Girls can't own their own land."

"Not fair at all,"
said Mahlah.

"That's not fair!"
said Tirzah.

The five sisters marched straight to Moses. They stood side by side, in front of the Tabernacle. "It's not right that we can't keep this land for ourselves, just because we are girls!" Milcah said to him. "Our father had no sons. Should his land just be lost?"

Moses took their question to God and asked, "What do I do? How should I solve their case?"

"The sisters are right," God said. "Make a change to the law, and give the sisters their fair share of the land."

The sisters beamed with happiness. They could build their house together and be a family. But even more, the sisters felt proud—they changed the law to be fairer for everyone.

29

Moses Hit the Rock

"We're so thirsty, Moses! What are we going to do?" complained the Israelites. In the middle of the dry, hot desert, the people couldn't find any water. "We've looked everywhere, and there's not a drop to drink!"

Moses didn't know what to do, so he asked God.

God answered, "Take your staff, and gather the whole community together by the big rock in the center of camp," said God. "Go speak to the rock, and tell it to give you water. Refreshing cold water will spring out for everyone to drink."

Moses asked all the people to stand with him by the big rock. But the people complained even more. "Moses, you'll never find us water to drink!" barked an Israelite, red in the face from the heat.

"What is this rock going to do for us? Nothing!" shouted another. "We should have stayed in Egypt! At least there we had water to drink!"

All their complaining frustrated Moses. Instead of speaking to the rock like God had instructed, Moses raised his staff in the air, and hit the rock. To everyone's surprise, water sprung from the rock. The people finally had water to drink, but God was upset with Moses for not following the directions.

"Moses, I know you are frustrated but you should have trusted me. I told you to talk to the rock, but you didn't believe that it would work," God said.

Moses realized that he made a mistake. Even leaders sometimes do the wrong thing. Next time, Moses would try to take a deep breath, remember to stay calm, and not let his frustration get in the way.

30

Lead Us to the Land

The Israelites had traveled through the desert for forty years. Finally, they stood on the banks of the Jordan River, ready to enter the land of Canaan. Moses had grown very old. The Israelites needed a new leader for the next chapter of their journey. Joshua was chosen.

Joshua felt nervous, like he had butterflies in his stomach. "Am I ready to be the leader of the Israelites?" he thought to himself. "Moses led us out of Egypt and through the wilderness all these years. He's the only leader we've ever known!"

Moses looked into Joshua's eyes and said, "You can do this, I believe in you. You've got what it takes to lead the people on this next big adventure."

As a last gift to his people, Moses finished writing down all their stories, adventures, and lessons in a very long scroll called a Torah.

"Keep this Torah safe, and bring it with you into your new home," Moses told Joshua. He rolled up the scroll and gave it to Joshua for safekeeping.

Moses climbed to the top of Mount Nebo and saw
Canaan stretched out in front of him. "Wow, look
at that," Moses said to himself. "It's everything I
hoped it would be. My people are home." He took
a deep breath and closed his eyes, remembering
how beautiful it looked.

At the base of the mountain, Joshua said, "Let's go, everyone! We've got a long, tiring day of walking ahead of us."

The Israelites packed their bags for the last time.

The journey through the wilderness had come to an end, and it was time for the Israelites to finally build a home of their own.

How to Bring the Stories to Life

How can you help ignite the imagination of a young child when reading these stories? Here are a few tips for ways to bring this book to life as you read:

- **Find a cozy spot and focus on each other.** Create dedicated time to read. Put away your phone or any other distractions.

- **Pause to look at the illustrations and invite description.** Ask your child: What do you notice in the picture? What part of the story does it show? What else do you imagine beyond the illustration here?

- **Invite your child to add sound and other details to the story.** For example, if a story includes a storm, try to make the sounds of the storm together using your voices or other objects in the room.

- **Build the world of the story and act it out.** Use toys and other items from around the house to create the scene. For example, build Noah's ark out of bed sheets, chairs, and couch cushions. Act out a moment from the story together.

- **Ask questions.** After you finish reading, ask your child about the story. You can discuss your favorite part or what you think will happen next. Ask your child to share their thoughts about the story and listen to what they have to say.

About the Author

Jonathan Shmidt Chapman is an award-winning artist, writer, and Jewish educator. He is the author of *Let There Be Play: Bringing the Bible to Life with Young Children.* Jonathan's theatrical work has been presented by Lincoln Center for the Performing Arts, the Kennedy Center, and Seattle Children's Theatre. He lives in the Chicago area with his husband, Rabbi David Chapman, and their two children, Elior and Amitai.

About the Illustrator

César Garcés graduated with a degree in graphic design from the Universidad Nacional Autónoma de México. He loves illustrating for children and has illustrated several picture books. He enjoys traveling, music, and spending time with family and friends. He lives in Mexico City.